Wireless Networks
Passwords

Location:

Wireless Network:

Password:

Location:

Wireless Network:

Password:

Location:

Wireless Network:

Password:

Location:

Wireless Network:

Password:

Location:

Wireless Network:

Password:

A

Account:

Username:

Password:

Email:

Pin Code:

Security Question:

Account:

Username:

Password:

Email:

Pin Code:

Security Question:

Account:

Username:

Password:

Email:

Pin Code:

Security Question:

Account:

Username:

Password:

Email:

Pin Code:

Security Question:

Account:

Username:

Password:

Email:

Pin Code:

Security Question:

Account:

Username:

Password:

Email:

Pin Code:

Security Question:

A |

Account:

Username:

Password:

Email:

Pin Code:

Security Question:

Account:

Username:

Password:

Email:

Pin Code:

Security Question:

Account:

Username:

Password:

Email:

Pin Code:

Security Question:

_____

Account: _____

Username: _____

Password: _____

Email: _____

Pin Code: _____

Security Question: _____

_____

_____

Account: _____

Username: _____

Password: _____

Email: _____

Pin Code: _____

Security Question: _____

_____

_____

Account: _____

Username: _____

Password: _____

Email: _____

Pin Code: _____

Security Question: _____

_____

_____

B

Account:

Username:

Password:

Email:

Pin Code:

Security Question:

Account:

Username:

Password:

Email:

Pin Code:

Security Question:

Account:

Username:

Password:

Email:

Pin Code:

Security Question:

Account:

Username:

Password:

Email:

Pin Code:

Security Question:

Account:

Username:

Password:

Email:

Pin Code:

Security Question:

Account:

Username:

Password:

Email:

Pin Code:

Security Question:

B

Account:

Username:

Password:

Email:

Pin Code:

Security Question:

Account:

Username:

Password:

Email:

Pin Code:

Security Question:

Account:

Username:

Password:

Email:

Pin Code:

Security Question:

Account:

Username:

Password:

Email:

Pin Code:

Security Question:

Account:

Username:

Password:

Email:

Pin Code:

Security Question:

Account:

Username:

Password:

Email:

Pin Code:

Security Question:

C

Account:

Username:

Password:

Email:

Pin Code:

Security Question:

Account:

Username:

Password:

Email:

Pin Code:

Security Question:

Account:

Username:

Password:

Email:

Pin Code:

Security Question:

Account:

Username:

Password:

Email:

Pin Code:

Security Question:

Account:

Username:

Password:

Email:

Pin Code:

Security Question:

Account:

Username:

Password:

Email:

Pin Code:

Security Question:

C

Account:
_____
Username:
_____
Password:
_____
Email:
_____
Pin Code:
_____
Security Question:
_____

_____

Account:
_____
Username:
_____
Password:
_____
Email:
_____
Pin Code:
_____
Security Question:
_____

_____

Account:
_____
Username:
_____
Password:
_____
Email:
_____
Pin Code:
_____
Security Question:
_____

_____

Account:

Username:

Password:

Email:

Pin Code:

Security Question:

Account:

Username:

Password:

Email:

Pin Code:

Security Question:

Account:

Username:

Password:

Email:

Pin Code:

Security Question:

D

Account:

Username:

Password:

Email:

Pin Code:

Security Question:

Account:

Username:

Password:

Email:

Pin Code:

Security Question:

Account:

Username:

Password:

Email:

Pin Code:

Security Question:

Account:

Username:

Password:

Email:

Pin Code:

Security Question:

Account:

Username:

Password:

Email:

Pin Code:

Security Question:

Account:

Username:

Password:

Email:

Pin Code:

Security Question:

D

Account:

Username:

Password:

Email:

Pin Code:

Security Question:

Account:

Username:

Password:

Email:

Pin Code:

Security Question:

Account:

Username:

Password:

Email:

Pin Code:

Security Question:

Account: _____

Username: _____

Password: _____

Email: _____

Pin Code: _____

Security Question: _____

_____

_____

Account: _____

Username: _____

Password: _____

Email: _____

Pin Code: _____

Security Question: _____

_____

_____

Account: _____

Username: _____

Password: _____

Email: _____

Pin Code: _____

Security Question: _____

_____

_____

E

Account:
_____

Username:
_____

Password:
_____

Email:
_____

Pin Code:
_____

Security Question:
_____

_____

Account:
_____

Username:
_____

Password:
_____

Email:
_____

Pin Code:
_____

Security Question:
_____

_____

Account:
_____

Username:
_____

Password:
_____

Email:
_____

Pin Code:
_____

Security Question:
_____

_____

Account: _____

Username: _____

Password: _____

Email: _____

Pin Code: _____

Security Question: _____

_____

_____

Account: _____

Username: _____

Password: _____

Email: _____

Pin Code: _____

Security Question: _____

_____

_____

Account: _____

Username: _____

Password: _____

Email: _____

Pin Code: _____

Security Question: _____

_____

_____

E

Account:

Username:

Password:

Email:

Pin Code:

Security Question:

Account:

Username:

Password:

Email:

Pin Code:

Security Question:

Account:

Username:

Password:

Email:

Pin Code:

Security Question:

Account:

Username:

Password:

Email:

Pin Code:

Security Question:

Account:

Username:

Password:

Email:

Pin Code:

Security Question:

Account:

Username:

Password:

Email:

Pin Code:

Security Question:

F

Account:

Username:

Password:

Email:

Pin Code:

Security Question:

Account:

Username:

Password:

Email:

Pin Code:

Security Question:

Account:

Username:

Password:

Email:

Pin Code:

Security Question:

Account:

Username:

Password:

Email:

Pin Code:

Security Question:

Account:

Username:

Password:

Email:

Pin Code:

Security Question:

Account:

Username:

Password:

Email:

Pin Code:

Security Question:

F

Account: _____

Username: _____

Password: _____

Email: _____

Pin Code: _____

Security Question: _____

_____

_____

Account: _____

Username: _____

Password: _____

Email: _____

Pin Code: _____

Security Question: _____

_____

_____

Account: _____

Username: _____

Password: _____

Email: _____

Pin Code: _____

Security Question: _____

_____

_____

Account: _____

Username: _____

Password: _____

Email: _____

Pin Code: _____

Security Question: _____

_____

_____

Account: _____

Username: _____

Password: _____

Email: _____

Pin Code: _____

Security Question: _____

_____

_____

Account: _____

Username: _____

Password: _____

Email: _____

Pin Code: _____

Security Question: _____

_____

_____

G

Account:

Username:

Password:

Email:

Pin Code:

Security Question:

Account:

Username:

Password:

Email:

Pin Code:

Security Question:

Account:

Username:

Password:

Email:

Pin Code:

Security Question:

Account:

Username:

Password:

Email:

Pin Code:

Security Question:

Account:

Username:

Password:

Email:

Pin Code:

Security Question:

Account:

Username:

Password:

Email:

Pin Code:

Security Question:

G

Account:

Username:

Password:

Email:

Pin Code:

Security Question:

Account:

Username:

Password:

Email:

Pin Code:

Security Question:

Account:

Username:

Password:

Email:

Pin Code:

Security Question:

Account: _____

Username: _____

Password: _____

Email: _____

Pin Code: _____

Security Question: _____

_____

_____

Account: _____

Username: _____

Password: _____

Email: _____

Pin Code: _____

Security Question: _____

_____

_____

Account: _____

Username: _____

Password: _____

Email: _____

Pin Code: _____

Security Question: _____

_____

_____

H

Account:
_____

Username:
_____

Password:
_____

Email:
_____

Pin Code:
_____

Security Question:
_____

_____

_____

Account:
_____

Username:
_____

Password:
_____

Email:
_____

Pin Code:
_____

Security Question:
_____

_____

_____

Account:
_____

Username:
_____

Password:
_____

Email:
_____

Pin Code:
_____

Security Question:
_____

_____

_____

Account:

Username:

Password:

Email:

Pin Code:

Security Question:

Account:

Username:

Password:

Email:

Pin Code:

Security Question:

Account:

Username:

Password:

Email:

Pin Code:

Security Question:

H

Account:

Username:

Password:

Email:

Pin Code:

Security Question:

Account:

Username:

Password:

Email:

Pin Code:

Security Question:

Account:

Username:

Password:

Email:

Pin Code:

Security Question:

Account:

Username:

Password:

Email:

Pin Code:

Security Question:

Account:

Username:

Password:

Email:

Pin Code:

Security Question:

Account:

Username:

Password:

Email:

Pin Code:

Security Question:

I

Account:

Username:

Password:

Email:

Pin Code:

Security Question:

Account:

Username:

Password:

Email:

Pin Code:

Security Question:

Account:

Username:

Password:

Email:

Pin Code:

Security Question:

Account:

Username:

Password:

Email:

Pin Code:

Security Question:

Account:

Username:

Password:

Email:

Pin Code:

Security Question:

Account:

Username:

Password:

Email:

Pin Code:

Security Question:

I |_____

Account: _____

Username: _____

Password: _____

Email: _____

Pin Code: _____

Security Question: _____

_____

_____

Account: _____

Username: _____

Password: _____

Email: _____

Pin Code: _____

Security Question: _____

_____

_____

Account: _____

Username: _____

Password: _____

Email: _____

Pin Code: _____

Security Question: _____

_____

_____

Account:

Username:

Password:

Email:

Pin Code:

Security Question:

Account:

Username:

Password:

Email:

Pin Code:

Security Question:

Account:

Username:

Password:

Email:

Pin Code:

Security Question:

J

Account:

Username:

Password:

Email:

Pin Code:

Security Question:

Account:

Username:

Password:

Email:

Pin Code:

Security Question:

Account:

Username:

Password:

Email:

Pin Code:

Security Question:

Account:

Username:

Password:

Email:

Pin Code:

Security Question:

Account:

Username:

Password:

Email:

Pin Code:

Security Question:

Account:

Username:

Password:

Email:

Pin Code:

Security Question:

J

Account:

Username:

Password:

Email:

Pin Code:

Security Question:

Account:

Username:

Password:

Email:

Pin Code:

Security Question:

Account:

Username:

Password:

Email:

Pin Code:

Security Question:

Account:

Username:

Password:

Email:

Pin Code:

Security Question:

Account:

Username:

Password:

Email:

Pin Code:

Security Question:

Account:

Username:

Password:

Email:

Pin Code:

Security Question:

K

Account:

Username:

Password:

Email:

Pin Code:

Security Question:

Account:

Username:

Password:

Email:

Pin Code:

Security Question:

Account:

Username:

Password:

Email:

Pin Code:

Security Question:

_____

Account:
_____
Username:
_____
Password:
_____
Email:
_____
Pin Code:
_____
Security Question:
_____
_____
_____

Account:
_____
Username:
_____
Password:
_____
Email:
_____
Pin Code:
_____
Security Question:
_____
_____
_____

Account:
_____
Username:
_____
Password:
_____
Email:
_____
Pin Code:
_____
Security Question:
_____
_____
_____

K

Account:

Username:

Password:

Email:

Pin Code:

Security Question:

Account:

Username:

Password:

Email:

Pin Code:

Security Question:

Account:

Username:

Password:

Email:

Pin Code:

Security Question:

Account:

Username:

Password:

Email:

Pin Code:

Security Question:

Account:

Username:

Password:

Email:

Pin Code:

Security Question:

Account:

Username:

Password:

Email:

Pin Code:

Security Question:

L

Account:

Username:

Password:

Email:

Pin Code:

Security Question:

Account:

Username:

Password:

Email:

Pin Code:

Security Question:

Account:

Username:

Password:

Email:

Pin Code:

Security Question:

_____

Account: _____

Username: _____

Password: _____

Email: _____

Pin Code: _____

Security Question: _____

_____

_____

Account: _____

Username: _____

Password: _____

Email: _____

Pin Code: _____

Security Question: _____

_____

_____

Account: _____

Username: _____

Password: _____

Email: _____

Pin Code: _____

Security Question: _____

_____

_____

L |

Account:
_____
Username:
_____
Password:
_____
Email:
_____
Pin Code:
_____
Security Question:
_____

_____

Account:
_____
Username:
_____
Password:
_____
Email:
_____
Pin Code:
_____
Security Question:
_____

_____

Account:
_____
Username:
_____
Password:
_____
Email:
_____
Pin Code:
_____
Security Question:
_____

_____

Account:

Username:

Password:

Email:

Pin Code:

Security Question:

Account:

Username:

Password:

Email:

Pin Code:

Security Question:

Account:

Username:

Password:

Email:

Pin Code:

Security Question:

M

Account: _____

Username: _____

Password: _____

Email: _____

Pin Code: _____

Security Question: _____

_____

_____

Account: _____

Username: _____

Password: _____

Email: _____

Pin Code: _____

Security Question: _____

_____

_____

Account: _____

Username: _____

Password: _____

Email: _____

Pin Code: _____

Security Question: _____

_____

_____

Account:

Username:

Password:

Email:

Pin Code:

Security Question:

Account:

Username:

Password:

Email:

Pin Code:

Security Question:

Account:

Username:

Password:

Email:

Pin Code:

Security Question:

M |

Account:

Username:

Password:

Email:

Pin Code:

Security Question:

Account:

Username:

Password:

Email:

Pin Code:

Security Question:

Account:

Username:

Password:

Email:

Pin Code:

Security Question:

Account:

Username:

Password:

Email:

Pin Code:

Security Question:

Account:

Username:

Password:

Email:

Pin Code:

Security Question:

Account:

Username:

Password:

Email:

Pin Code:

Security Question:

N

Account:

Username:

Password:

Email:

Pin Code:

Security Question:

Account:

Username:

Password:

Email:

Pin Code:

Security Question:

Account:

Username:

Password:

Email:

Pin Code:

Security Question:

Account:

Username:

Password:

Email:

Pin Code:

Security Question:

Account:

Username:

Password:

Email:

Pin Code:

Security Question:

Account:

Username:

Password:

Email:

Pin Code:

Security Question:

N |

Account: _____

Username: _____

Password: _____

Email: _____

Pin Code: _____

Security Question: _____

_____

_____

Account: _____

Username: _____

Password: _____

Email: _____

Pin Code: _____

Security Question: _____

_____

_____

Account: _____

Username: _____

Password: _____

Email: _____

Pin Code: _____

Security Question: _____

_____

_____

Account: _____

Username: _____

Password: _____

Email: _____

Pin Code: _____

Security Question: _____

_____

_____

Account: _____

Username: _____

Password: _____

Email: _____

Pin Code: _____

Security Question: _____

_____

_____

Account: _____

Username: _____

Password: _____

Email: _____

Pin Code: _____

Security Question: _____

_____

_____

O

Account:

Username:

Password:

Email:

Pin Code:

Security Question:

Account:

Username:

Password:

Email:

Pin Code:

Security Question:

Account:

Username:

Password:

Email:

Pin Code:

Security Question:

Account:

Username:

Password:

Email:

Pin Code:

Security Question:

Account:

Username:

Password:

Email:

Pin Code:

Security Question:

Account:

Username:

Password:

Email:

Pin Code:

Security Question:

O

Account:

Username:

Password:

Email:

Pin Code:

Security Question:

Account:

Username:

Password:

Email:

Pin Code:

Security Question:

Account:

Username:

Password:

Email:

Pin Code:

Security Question:

Account:

Username:

Password:

Email:

Pin Code:

Security Question:

Account:

Username:

Password:

Email:

Pin Code:

Security Question:

Account:

Username:

Password:

Email:

Pin Code:

Security Question:

P

Account: _____

Username: _____

Password: _____

Email: _____

Pin Code: _____

Security Question: _____

_____

_____

Account: _____

Username: _____

Password: _____

Email: _____

Pin Code: _____

Security Question: _____

_____

_____

Account: _____

Username: _____

Password: _____

Email: _____

Pin Code: _____

Security Question: _____

_____

_____

Account:

Username:

Password:

Email:

Pin Code:

Security Question:

Account:

Username:

Password:

Email:

Pin Code:

Security Question:

Account:

Username:

Password:

Email:

Pin Code:

Security Question:

P

Account:

Username:

Password:

Email:

Pin Code:

Security Question:

Account:

Username:

Password:

Email:

Pin Code:

Security Question:

Account:

Username:

Password:

Email:

Pin Code:

Security Question:

Account:

Username:

Password:

Email:

Pin Code:

Security Question:

Account:

Username:

Password:

Email:

Pin Code:

Security Question:

Account:

Username:

Password:

Email:

Pin Code:

Security Question:

Q

Account:

Username:

Password:

Email:

Pin Code:

Security Question:

Account:

Username:

Password:

Email:

Pin Code:

Security Question:

Account:

Username:

Password:

Email:

Pin Code:

Security Question:

Account:

Username:

Password:

Email:

Pin Code:

Security Question:

Account:

Username:

Password:

Email:

Pin Code:

Security Question:

Account:

Username:

Password:

Email:

Pin Code:

Security Question:

Q

Account:

Username:

Password:

Email:

Pin Code:

Security Question:

Account:

Username:

Password:

Email:

Pin Code:

Security Question:

Account:

Username:

Password:

Email:

Pin Code:

Security Question:

Account:

Username:

Password:

Email:

Pin Code:

Security Question:

Account:

Username:

Password:

Email:

Pin Code:

Security Question:

Account:

Username:

Password:

Email:

Pin Code:

Security Question:

R

Account:
_____

Username:
_____

Password:
_____

Email:
_____

Pin Code:
_____

Security Question:
_____

_____

_____

Account:
_____

Username:
_____

Password:
_____

Email:
_____

Pin Code:
_____

Security Question:
_____

_____

_____

Account:
_____

Username:
_____

Password:
_____

Email:
_____

Pin Code:
_____

Security Question:
_____

_____

_____

Account:

Username:

Password:

Email:

Pin Code:

Security Question:

Account:

Username:

Password:

Email:

Pin Code:

Security Question:

Account:

Username:

Password:

Email:

Pin Code:

Security Question:

R

Account:

Username:

Password:

Email:

Pin Code:

Security Question:

Account:

Username:

Password:

Email:

Pin Code:

Security Question:

Account:

Username:

Password:

Email:

Pin Code:

Security Question:

Account:

Username:

Password:

Email:

Pin Code:

Security Question:

Account:

Username:

Password:

Email:

Pin Code:

Security Question:

Account:

Username:

Password:

Email:

Pin Code:

Security Question:

S

Account:
_____

Username:
_____

Password:
_____

Email:
_____

Pin Code:
_____

Security Question:
_____

_____

_____

Account:
_____

Username:
_____

Password:
_____

Email:
_____

Pin Code:
_____

Security Question:
_____

_____

_____

Account:
_____

Username:
_____

Password:
_____

Email:
_____

Pin Code:
_____

Security Question:
_____

_____

_____

Account:

Username:

Password:

Email:

Pin Code:

Security Question:

Account:

Username:

Password:

Email:

Pin Code:

Security Question:

Account:

Username:

Password:

Email:

Pin Code:

Security Question:

S

Account:

Username:

Password:

Email:

Pin Code:

Security Question:

Account:

Username:

Password:

Email:

Pin Code:

Security Question:

Account:

Username:

Password:

Email:

Pin Code:

Security Question:

Account:

Username:

Password:

Email:

Pin Code:

Security Question:

Account:

Username:

Password:

Email:

Pin Code:

Security Question:

Account:

Username:

Password:

Email:

Pin Code:

Security Question:

T |_____

Account:
_____

Username:
_____

Password:
_____

Email:
_____

Pin Code:
_____

Security Question:
_____

_____

_____

Account:
_____

Username:
_____

Password:
_____

Email:
_____

Pin Code:
_____

Security Question:
_____

_____

_____

Account:
_____

Username:
_____

Password:
_____

Email:
_____

Pin Code:
_____

Security Question:
_____

_____

_____

Account:

Username:

Password:

Email:

Pin Code:

Security Question:

Account:

Username:

Password:

Email:

Pin Code:

Security Question:

Account:

Username:

Password:

Email:

Pin Code:

Security Question:

T |_____

Account: _____

Username: _____

Password: _____

Email: _____

Pin Code: _____

Security Question: _____

_____

_____

Account: _____

Username: _____

Password: _____

Email: _____

Pin Code: _____

Security Question: _____

_____

_____

Account: _____

Username: _____

Password: _____

Email: _____

Pin Code: _____

Security Question: _____

_____

_____

Account:
_____

Username:
_____

Password:
_____

Email:
_____

Pin Code:
_____

Security Question:
_____

_____

_____

Account:
_____

Username:
_____

Password:
_____

Email:
_____

Pin Code:
_____

Security Question:
_____

_____

_____

Account:
_____

Username:
_____

Password:
_____

Email:
_____

Pin Code:
_____

Security Question:
_____

_____

_____

U

Account:

Username:

Password:

Email:

Pin Code:

Security Question:

Account:

Username:

Password:

Email:

Pin Code:

Security Question:

Account:

Username:

Password:

Email:

Pin Code:

Security Question:

Account:

Username:

Password:

Email:

Pin Code:

Security Question:

Account:

Username:

Password:

Email:

Pin Code:

Security Question:

Account:

Username:

Password:

Email:

Pin Code:

Security Question:

U

Account:

Username:

Password:

Email:

Pin Code:

Security Question:

Account:

Username:

Password:

Email:

Pin Code:

Security Question:

Account:

Username:

Password:

Email:

Pin Code:

Security Question:

Account:

Username:

Password:

Email:

Pin Code:

Security Question:

Account:

Username:

Password:

Email:

Pin Code:

Security Question:

Account:

Username:

Password:

Email:

Pin Code:

Security Question:

V _____

Account: _____

Username: _____

Password: _____

Email: _____

Pin Code: _____

Security Question: _____

_____

_____

Account: _____

Username: _____

Password: _____

Email: _____

Pin Code: _____

Security Question: _____

_____

_____

Account: _____

Username: _____

Password: _____

Email: _____

Pin Code: _____

Security Question: _____

_____

_____

Account:

Username:

Password:

Email:

Pin Code:

Security Question:

Account:

Username:

Password:

Email:

Pin Code:

Security Question:

Account:

Username:

Password:

Email:

Pin Code:

Security Question:

V

Account: _____

Username: _____

Password: _____

Email: _____

Pin Code: _____

Security Question: _____

_____

_____

Account: _____

Username: _____

Password: _____

Email: _____

Pin Code: _____

Security Question: _____

_____

_____

Account: _____

Username: _____

Password: _____

Email: _____

Pin Code: _____

Security Question: _____

_____

_____

Account:

Username:

Password:

Email:

Pin Code:

Security Question:

Account:

Username:

Password:

Email:

Pin Code:

Security Question:

Account:

Username:

Password:

Email:

Pin Code:

Security Question:

W

Account:

Username:

Password:

Email:

Pin Code:

Security Question:

Account:

Username:

Password:

Email:

Pin Code:

Security Question:

Account:

Username:

Password:

Email:

Pin Code:

Security Question:

Account:

Username:

Password:

Email:

Pin Code:

Security Question:

Account:

Username:

Password:

Email:

Pin Code:

Security Question:

Account:

Username:

Password:

Email:

Pin Code:

Security Question:

W

Account: _____

Username: _____

Password: _____

Email: _____

Pin Code: _____

Security Question: _____

_____

_____

Account: _____

Username: _____

Password: _____

Email: _____

Pin Code: _____

Security Question: _____

_____

_____

Account: _____

Username: _____

Password: _____

Email: _____

Pin Code: _____

Security Question: _____

_____

_____

Account:

Username:

Password:

Email:

Pin Code:

Security Question:

Account:

Username:

Password:

Email:

Pin Code:

Security Question:

Account:

Username:

Password:

Email:

Pin Code:

Security Question:

XYZ

Account:

Username:

Password:

Email:

Pin Code:

Security Question:

Account:

Username:

Password:

Email:

Pin Code:

Security Question:

Account:

Username:

Password:

Email:

Pin Code:

Security Question:

Account:

Username:

Password:

Email:

Pin Code:

Security Question:

Account:

Username:

Password:

Email:

Pin Code:

Security Question:

Account:

Username:

Password:

Email:

Pin Code:

Security Question:

XYZ

Account:

Username:

Password:

Email:

Pin Code:

Security Question:

Account:

Username:

Password:

Email:

Pin Code:

Security Question:

Account:

Username:

Password:

Email:

Pin Code:

Security Question:

Account:

Username:

Password:

Email:

Pin Code:

Security Question:

Account:

Username:

Password:

Email:

Pin Code:

Security Question:

Account:

Username:

Password:

Email:

Pin Code:

Security Question: